T0390044

FERRARI

BY DALTON RAINS

Apex is distributed by North Star Editions:
sales@northstareditions.com | 888-417-0195

Produced for Apex by Red Line Editorial.

Photographs ©: Pexels, cover; iStockphoto, 1, 13, 14–15, 18–19; Mark Thompson/Getty Images Sport/Getty Images, 4–5; Rudy Carezzevoli/Getty Images Sport/Getty Images, 6–7; Clive Rose/Getty Images Sport/Getty Images, 8–9; AP Images, 10–11; Klemantaski Collection/Hulton Archive/Getty Images, 12; Shutterstock Images, 16–17, 20–21, 22–23, 24, 25, 29; Nippon News/Aflo Co. Ltd./Alamy Stock Photo, 26–27

Library of Congress Control Number: 2024952633

ISBN
979-8-89250-520-8 (hardcover)
979-8-89250-556-7 (paperback)
979-8-89250-627-4 (ebook pdf)
979-8-89250-592-5 (hosted ebook)

Printed in the United States of America
Mankato, MN
082025

NOTE TO PARENTS AND EDUCATORS

Apex books are designed to build literacy skills in striving readers. Exciting, high-interest content attracts and holds readers' attention. The text is carefully leveled to allow students to achieve success quickly. Additional features, such as bolded glossary words for difficult terms, help build comprehension.

TABLE OF CONTENTS

FIRST-PLACE FINISH

Charles Leclerc revs the engine of his Ferrari. A **Formula 1** race begins. It's the Italian **Grand Prix**. The Ferrari shoots down the track.

Charles Leclerc races his Ferrari during the 2024 Italian Grand Prix.

During Formula 1 races, a car's tires can wear out. Most drivers stop twice for repairs.

Leclerc zips around corners. He's stuck in the middle of the pack. One by one, the other cars take a second **pit stop**. But the Ferrari stays on the track.

FAST FACT

Most Formula 1 races are about 190 miles (305 km) long.

Finally, the Ferrari takes the lead. Leclerc flies past the finish line in first place.

LONG HISTORY

Ferrari has a tradition of great racing. The team has won many Formula 1 races. Ferrari even won six straight Formula 1 **championships** from 1999 to 2004.

Ferrari is based in Italy. That made Leclerc's win extra exciting for many fans there.

CHAPTER 2

HiSTORY

Enzo Ferrari started a racing team in 1929. It became very successful. Ferrari sold the team in the late 1930s. He used the money to build his own cars.

Enzo Ferrari began his career by testing and racing cars for other companies.

Franco Cortese races in a Ferrari 125 S in 1947. Cortese was Ferrari's first race car driver.

The Ferrari 125 S came out in 1947. It had a strong engine. That helped Ferrari win its first Grand Prix. The Ferrari 166 MM continued the success.

RARE CARS

Very few Ferrari 250 GTOs exist. Only 36 were ever made. They became one of the most-wanted cars for collectors. In 2023, a 250 GTO sold for more than $50 million.

Ferrari built the 250 GTO from 1962 to 1964.

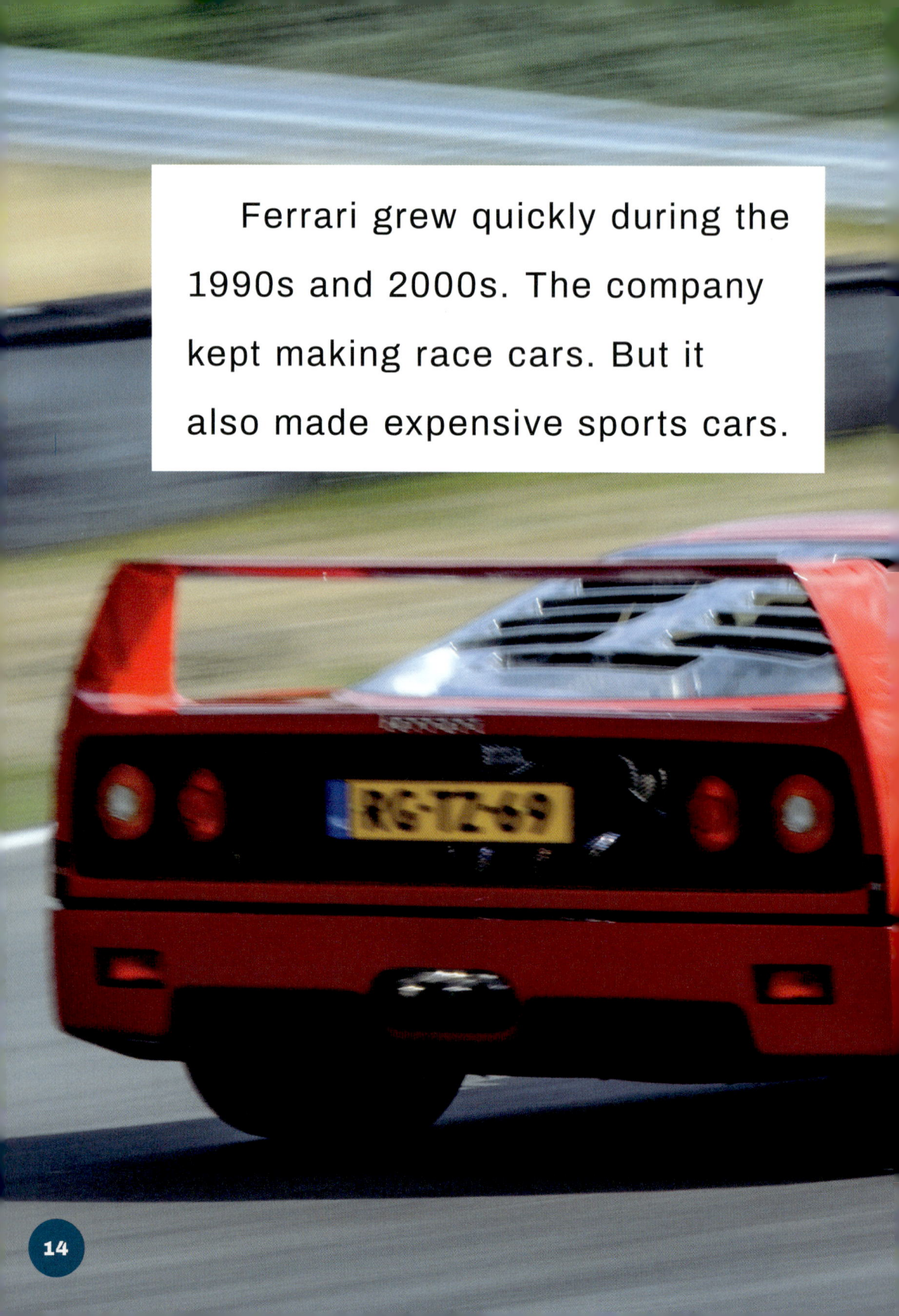

Ferrari grew quickly during the 1990s and 2000s. The company kept making race cars. But it also made expensive sports cars.

The Ferrari F40 was the first road car to top 200 miles per hour (322 km/h).

FAST FACT

Michael Schumacher was one of the greatest Formula 1 drivers. He raced for Ferrari from 1996 to 2006.

CHAPTER 3

FAST FERRARIS

Ferrari built many **iconic** cars. One was called the Enzo. The car featured sharp angles. It had a low, arrow-shaped nose. And it sported a new engine **design**.

The Enzo had Ferrari's most powerful V12 engine yet.

The 430 Scuderia was another popular car. It was lightweight. And it moved quickly. Many drivers liked the loud roar of its engine.

TEST DRIVES

Ferrari tests new models on racetracks. Michael Schumacher tested the Enzo and the 430 Scuderia. He helped the company make the sports cars similar to race cars.

The 430 Scuderia has a race mode. It helps the car make superfast turns.

A new LaFerrari cost $1.5 million.

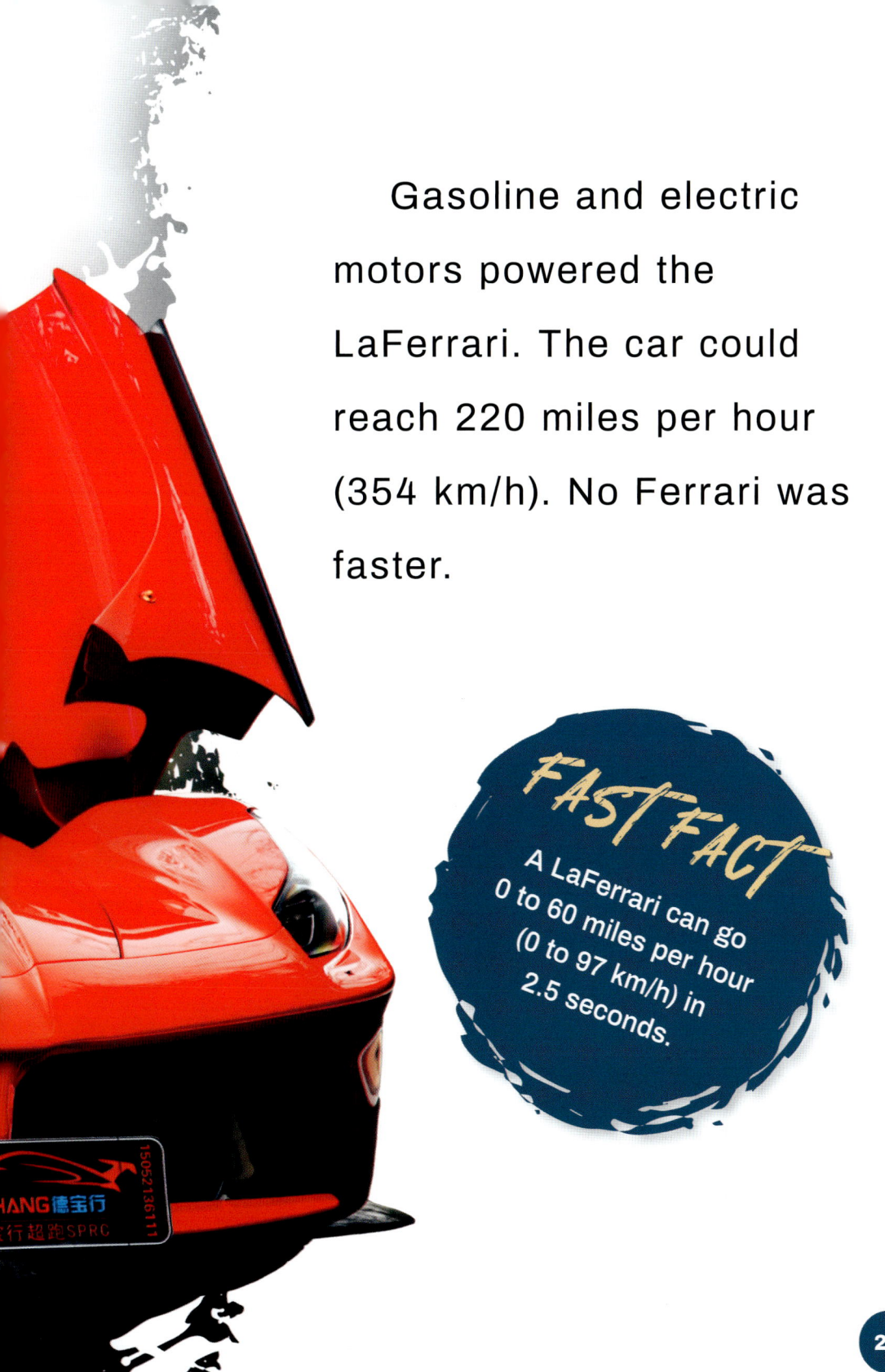

Gasoline and electric motors powered the LaFerrari. The car could reach 220 miles per hour (354 km/h). No Ferrari was faster.

FAST FACT

A LaFerrari can go 0 to 60 miles per hour (0 to 97 km/h) in 2.5 seconds.

CHAPTER 4

NEW CARS

n the early 2020s, Ferrari sold several main models. The Roma was the cheapest. But it still cost well over $200,000.

Ferrari named the Roma after the capital of Italy.
It showed its deep roots with the country.

The SF90 Stradale was Ferrari's first plug-in hybrid car.

Ferrari sold **plug-in hybrid** cars, too. The SF90 Stradale could top 210 miles per hour (338 km/h). The 296 GTB had a much smaller engine. But it still made drivers feel powerful.

FAST FACT

In 2022, Ferrari came out with the Purosangue. It was the first Ferrari with four doors.

People can charge the batteries of their SF90 Stradale or 296 GTB.

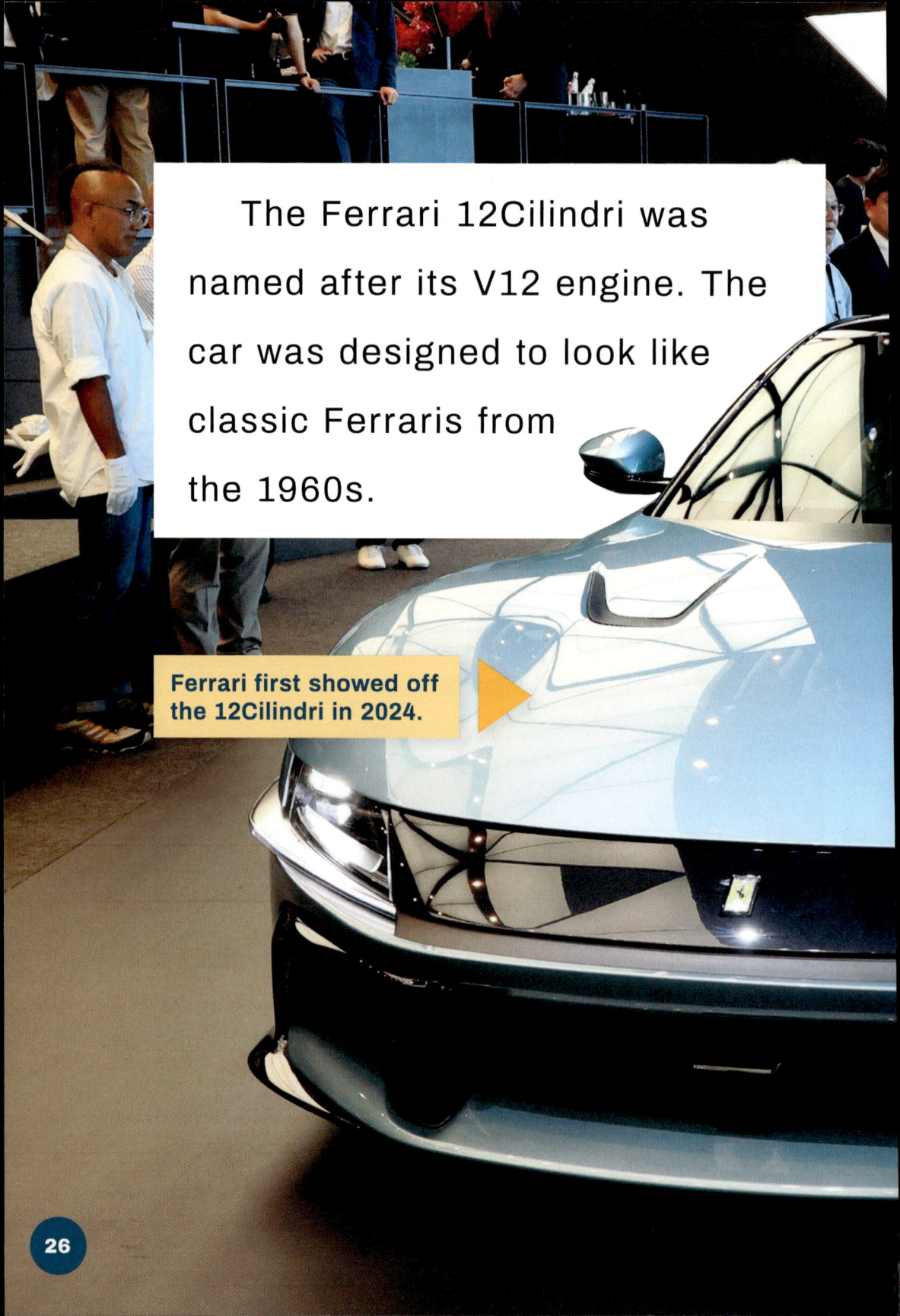

The Ferrari 12Cilindri was named after its V12 engine. The car was designed to look like classic Ferraris from the 1960s.

Ferrari first showed off the 12Cilindri in 2024.

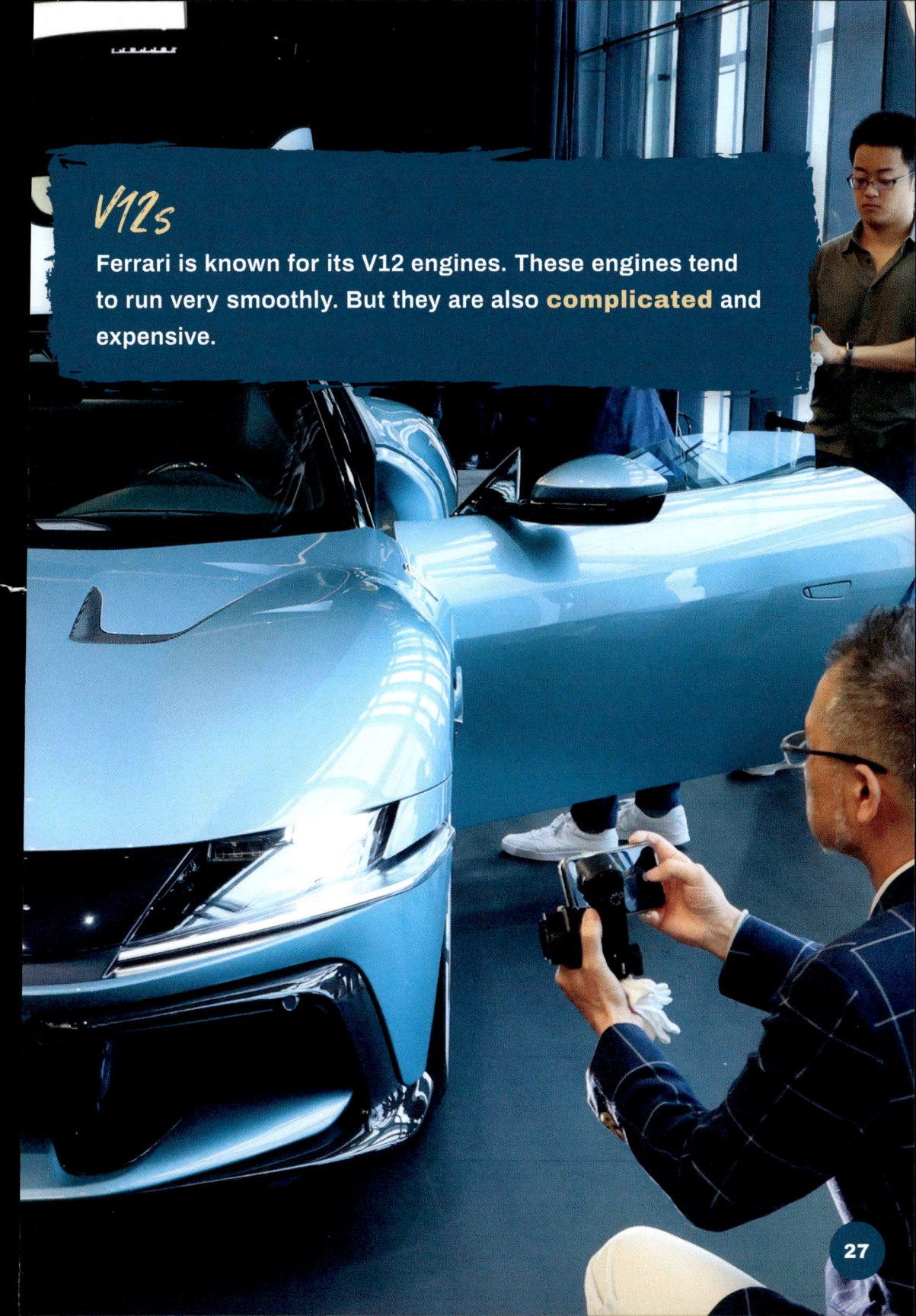

V12s

Ferrari is known for its V12 engines. These engines tend to run very smoothly. But they are also **complicated** and expensive.

COMPREHENSION
QUESTIONS

Write your answers on a separate piece of paper.

1. Write a few sentences explaining the main ideas of Chapter 3.

2. Which Ferrari model would you most like to ride in? Why?

3. When did the Ferrari 125 S come out?

    A. 1943

    B. 1947

    C. 1996

4. What helped Charles Leclerc win the Italian Grand Prix?

    A. He made just one pit stop during the race.

    B. He drove farther than other cars.

    C. He stopped for repairs more than other cars.

5. What does **tradition** mean in this book?

*Ferrari has a **tradition** of great racing. The team has won many Formula 1 races.*

    A. a surprising loss

    B. a one-time event

    C. a pattern over time

6. What does **motors** mean in this book?

*Gasoline and electric **motors** powered the LaFerrari. The car could reach 220 miles per hour (354 km/h).*

    A. machines that help something move

    B. ways to slow cars down

    C. laps left in a car race

Answer key on page 32.

GLOSSARY

championships
Contests that decide a winner.

complicated
Having many parts.

design
The way something looks or is made.

Formula 1
The highest level of open-wheel racing.

Grand Prix
A car race on a difficult course that is part of a world championship series.

iconic
Loved and recognized by many people.

pit stop
A time when race cars stop to get fuel or repairs.

plug-in hybrid
A car with both gasoline and electric motors. The car can charge its battery by plugging in to an outlet.

BOOKS

Duling, Kaitlyn. *Ferrari Roma*. Bellwether Media, 2025.

Hamilton, S. L. *Ferrari*. Abdo Publishing, 2023.

Rains, Dalton. *Formula 1 Racing*. Apex Editions, 2024.

ONLINE RESOURCES

Visit **www.apexeditions.com** to find links and resources related to this title.

ABOUT THE AUTHOR

Dalton Rains is a writer and editor from St. Paul, Minnesota. He would love to drive a Ferrari someday.

INDEX

ANSWER KEY:
1. Answers will vary; 2. Answers will vary; 3. B; 4. A; 5. C; 6. A